In the spring of 2011, my son was diagnosed with cluster headaches. The pain was extremely severe, as it shook his body and caused him to cry out. As a mother, I sat by his bedside, constantly praying that God would heal him. One night when it became unbearable for me to watch him suffer so severely, I went to my private place and began to pray. I cried out to God, *Please heal my son.* Very clearly and audibly, God spoke to me and said, *He is healed.* I immediately went and spoke these words to my son: "You are healed." Today my son is healed of cluster headaches that have been known to consume lives.

—Pecola Wiley, Elder
Family and Deaconess Ministries

I0108880

Applauding *Pray Powerfully*

I am an intercessor and have come to understand the importance of prayer. However, the true significance and the real power of intercessory prayer is best witnessed from the receiving end. It is from this perspective that I gain fuel to persist in prayer for others. Over the years, I have asked Elder Harriet to stand with me in prayer or to pray for me because I have confidence that she will pray fervently and effectually on my behalf, and I believe that her prayers have power.

—Janie Giles, Elder
Chief Intercessor

In a day and age when prayer is dismissed or disregarded, there remains a remnant of people who recognize its power. Through prayer we welcome God's direction for our lives, His peace for our troubles and hope for our future. Once you experience the power of prayer, you can't help but revel in God's goodness and grace!

—Robin May
Licensed Professional Counselor and Life Coach

I have found that when I spend quality time in prayer and fully submit my will, knowledge, gifts, and talents to God, He gives amazing revelation and clarity of direction. I was working on a project and needed a solution. I had an idea that I tried, and it failed. After a prayer group session where I sought His wisdom, He revealed the solution to me. As long as I operate in my own will and strength, He gently awaits my invitation for help. When I submit, He opens the door of understanding, knowledge, and wisdom. The information was available all along, but I had to submit to His authority to receive it.

—Anita Richardson
Co-Pastor Christian Growth Ministries

My mother has taught me that prayer is a powerful weapon with which we as Christians have been equipped. In the hands of an irresponsible soldier, it is only a threat. But in the mouths of committed warriors, it is a powerful force! In her book, Harriet Gordon gives practical tips on how to incorporate prayer into our daily lives. I remember at a young age, my mother taught me that prayer is simply communication with our heavenly Father. The insightful tools she offers in this book are full of wisdom and are guaranteed to be life changing.

—Dawn Gordon Smith, M.Ed.
Educator and Dance Choreographer

HARRIET GORDON, LPC

PEEL

PRAY POWERFULLY

NO BRANCH CAN BEAR FRUIT BY ITSELF;
IT MUST REMAIN ON THE VINE.
JOHN 15:4B

DISCLAIMER

The information presented herein is in no way intended as a substitute for medical counseling. This book was written to provide experiential information. Neither Harriet Gordon, GHD Inc., nor any member of the organization's board shall have liability or responsibility to any person with respect to damage, injury, or any alleged causes resulting from information in this book.

GOD'S DIVINE HANDIWORK, INC.

Our organization's goal is to affect the lives of people in the communities which we serve. God's Divine Handiwork, Inc. (GHDI), is a family-oriented organization which has deep concern for the well-being of our society. We desire to see people "well" in all aspects of their lives. We aim to educate society regarding academic, spiritual, emotional, and physical health. Conferences, forums, seminars, classes, and workshops may be arranged for your specific needs. Our services include courses entitled, but not limited to:

Healthy Living
Test-Taking Tips
Time Management
Parenting to the End
PEEL, Volume 1: *Pray Powerfully*
PEEL, Volume 2: *Eat Efficiently*
PEEL, Volume 3: *Exercise Enthusiastically*
PEEL, Volume 4: *Learn, Laugh, & Live Lovingly*
PEEL, Volume 5: *Cook Consciously*

**Contact us at peelv5@gmail.com
and on facebook at
http://www.facebook.com/peelv5**

"

It's the quality of your days rather than the quantity of your years that really counts. Enjoy life!

"

—Harriet Gordon, LPC

DEDICATION

PEEL, Volume 1: *Pray Powerfully* is dedicated to pastors who have dedicated their lives to making disciples of men.

To my family, who give me support and unconditional love.

Dedicated to my *mother*, Mary Esther West Burks.
I love her infinitely.

CONTENTS

ACKNOWLEDGMENTS

Light of the World Christian Tabernacle (family),
Stockbridge, Georgia;

Founder: the late Archbishop Jimmie L. Smith,
and Senior Pastor Dr. Ruth W. Smith Holmes,
Archbishop

The late Apostle Carol Rawls Davis,
Phenomenal Intercessors' Intercessor:
My *teacher* and *friend*

Whiteoak Grove Baptist Church family, Thomson,
Georgia

Bishop Belinda Campbell

My husband—Glenn D. Gordon
Our son—Glenn Isaac Gordon, II
Our daughter and family
—Jeremiah, Dawn, Jamari, and Gian Smith

1

Harriet Gordon, LPC

FOREWORD

What a milestone to have the first volume of *P.E.E.L.* in our hands. Volume 1 of *P.E.E.L.*, *Pray Powerfully*, will help one to establish a prayer life, which is foundational to spiritual development. *Pray Powerfully* has the potential to create a wave of revival that can only be birthed through prayer.

During our prayer time, which includes both speaking and listening to God, we have the opportunity to receive revelation that will help us in every area of our lives. Prayer helps us to learn to trust God, as faith is built, when we ask God for an answer and He responds. Hebrews 11:6 lets us know that without faith, it's impossible to please God.

Harriet Gordon, LPC, makes it clear in *P.E.E.L.* that prayer is not an option but a command. She further lays out the types of prayers, which are very critical in getting the results that we need. One type of prayer she expounds on is the prayer of thanksgiving. God loves a grateful and thankful heart, therefore the prayer of thanksgiving can keep us grounded through tough times.

P.E.E.L. Volume 1, *Pray Powerfully*, is not a book to simply read, but one to study. To get the most out of it, I encourage you to purchase a copy for yourself and each person on your team, and study it together. Discuss the benefits of a powerful prayer life, and make every effort to be a praying team. So go for it! My prayer is, "The Lord bless you and keep you; the Lord make His face shine upon you, and be gracious to you; the Lord lift up His countenance upon you, and give you peace" (Numbers 6:24–26 NKJV).

—Ruth Smith Holmes, Archbishop
Senior Pastor, Light of the World Christian
Tabernacle International

PREFACE

Community leaders, pastors, and individuals who desire to empower others and themselves will be blessed by this book. This is the first in a series of self-help publications designed to unleash the dormant power that is within. Prayer can break strongholds in geographical regions and individual lives. Prayer can turn generational curses into generational blessings.

A few months into the grief process after the death of a personal friend and coworker, the voice of the Lord spoke audibly to me. I knew grieving was a process, so I allowed myself to have my cathartic time before obeying the voice: "Hurry up. Get healed so you can help!" It was time to reach a broader audience. As an educator, only prayer and meditation helped me to overcome grief and maintain positive working relationships. As a minister, it is difficult to minister joy to others when you are suffering in silence. Finally, family is my heartbeat. It is impossible to exude healthy nurturing if you are unhealthy. On a daily basis, I found myself wearing masks as an educator, minister, wife, or mother. I desired more than anything else to be free!

James 5:16b tells us, "The effectual fervent prayer of a righteous man availeth much." A complete transformation was in the making, and my vibrant personality was returning. The anointing through powerful prayers from others and to the Lord delivered me.

This is the first of a series, and prayer is the key component in the equation. However, other parts are also important. For total victory, implement the advice from each volume:

P.   Pray Powerfully—Volume 1

E.   Eat Efficiently—Volume 2

E.   Exercise Enthusiastically—Volume 3

L.   Learn, Laugh, and Live Lovingly—Volume 4

INTRODUCTION

Is your contentment dial turned up to maximum capacity? Do you want to live a healthy and victorious life? The key is being good to your body, mind, and soul. Technological advancements in medicine and science make it possible for you to remain in excellent health. First, identify areas in your life which need improvement. You may find it necessary to rid yourself of things, habits, or even people. The mask of pretense will be destroyed, and you will be freed of guilt and pain in the process. Prayer is the foundation for a believer's spiritual development. God has provided various means of grace whereby the believer may avail himself of divine strength *to be* and power *to do*. This means those "divinely appointed channels" through which the Holy Spirit provides divine grace for Christian life and service. The two major channels of grace are the Word of God and **prayer.**

Power manifests by way of the Holy Spirit. When we are able to do what we cannot under normal circumstances, that is the Holy Spirit helping us. He works through us and is in the hearts of all believers.

Prayer teaches us to wait and be patient. Sometimes manifestations come over time; other times, we can pray and get full manifestation of prayers answered instantly. God is awesome—He gives us the power and the prayer to pray, then turns around and answers it! God knows our requests before we ask them. He hears and answers prayer.

One example: Indications show that holiday seasons and cold weather are stressors and contributing factors for various levels of depression. As a therapist, I interject that what is sometimes identified as having a "bad day" is actually depression. Depression may be classified as a mental illness, and when it becomes too difficult to get off the couch or to get out of bed, that is a huge RED light. Seek professional help!

I also note that ADL (Activities of Daily Living) represent the things you should be able to do to function normally in society. Simple tasks such as taking care of personal hygiene or operating a motor vehicle are included. However, powerful prayer can peel away depression or any stronghold that the enemy tries to put on you. That is my personal testimony.

Prayer may be defined as *removing masks and peeling away the guilt and pain of the past, persons, possessions, or professions. PRAY POWERFULLY and transform lives!* Remember, where we are strong, others may be weak; do not judge them. We can't judge others and live consecrated lives. Living a consecrated life, and knowing how and what to pray, are keys to answered prayer.

"

Powerful Prayer Promotes Productive Fruit!

"

Harriet Gordon, LPC

CHARACTERISTICS AND NATURE OF GENUINE PRAYER

As a classroom teacher, I established authority by setting guidelines for my students when they wanted to connect with me, receive my assistance, or make requests. They soon came to know my nature. Former students often commented how easy it was for me to get their attention. "You never yelled; you simply entered the room." Authority was established, and all they needed was my presence, because they knew my nature. Genuine prayer has characteristics and is a true power source. Incorporate these characteristics into your prayers to maintain a direct connection and exercise your authority

1. Through our prayer times, we learn more of God. He treats us as His children and wants to hear our requests. Through prayer, He is developing a deep

and enriching relationship with us. He wants us to realize how much He cares for us.

2. Prayer is two-way conversation between God and man.

3. Prayer reflects our trust that our Lord is able to move us from problem to prayer to praise.

4. We need to come to God through Jesus.

5. God wants to hear from us more often. Growing up with fathers who did not want to hear from us can affect our relationship with the Lord. We need to grow in our concept of God and prayer.

6. The Lord delights in hearing our thanks for His good gifts, which is a kind of prayer in itself. We should not be rude children who get what they demand but never give thanks. Because prayer is relational, it is a time to show appreciation.

7. If we properly understand singing and dancing before the Lord, we will see them as forms of prayer. There

are Psalms that lead us through wonderful times of worship as well as confession, or that help us during times of intense struggles and grief.

8. Confession or repentance before God are kinds of prayers. Many of us have not learned to bring our sins before God because we are afraid of rejection.

9. Requests are kinds of prayer. God wants to develop a constant growing relationship in our lives, and He does this partly through answering our personal prayers.

10. When we ask the Lord to do things on behalf of others, we are beginning to enter the heart of prayer; that is, completing God's will. We will be challenged to grow in our persistence as well as our faith when we intercede for others.

11. Prayer—two-way conversation—is also the place for meditation. We hear from God and want to talk to Him about what He says. During these times of reflection upon God and His Word, we learn to discern His thoughts as they enter our minds.

12. Prayer is the place where we discern God's voice, hear Him, and then *obey*. It is wisest to make important life decisions in our prayer times so that we are less affected by the evil one. This is a special training that many of us do not master. Satan infiltrates our spiritual discernment and interjects lies to get us to doubt and blame rather than trust God.

13. Prayer at best is a spiritual discipline in which we regularly engage the Lord and reflect on His Word. We cannot live on what we have eaten in the past, and likewise we need to regularly meet with the Lord for spiritual nourishment.

14. Since our prayers portray our beliefs, we can obtain a fairly accurate perspective by examining how we pray, what we pray, and how often or intensely we pray. We will see our strong and weak areas of life.

"
Prayer is the place where we discern God's voice, hear Him, and then obey. "

APPROACH

T he proper approach to prayer is to keep our motives pure. No one is better qualified to teach us how to pray than Jesus Himself. We often read of Him spending the night in prayer. Even on the night before His crucifixion, we find Jesus praying. This may have been one of the reasons His disciples asked Him, "Lord, teach us to pray" (Luke 11:1). His response is in what we now call "The Lord's Prayer" (Luke 11:2–4; Matthew 6:9–13). However, Jesus' longest prayer on record is John 17, when He prays right before His arrest.

You may wonder, "Is saying 'in Jesus' name' what it means to pray in His name?" Praying in Jesus' name means to pray His purpose and will. It means our prayers should reflect Jesus' purpose for our lives. In order to pray "in Jesus' name," our minds and hearts must reflect Scripture. To do this, we must set aside times of quiet to attend to the still, small voice of the Spirit of Jesus. When we pray in Jesus' name, not only are we approaching God in the authority of Jesus, but we are also coming with

Jesus' own desires. Approach the Father only under the authority of Jesus, only through what He has done for us on the cross. Our desire should be to bring our prayers more in line with what Jesus desires.

My mother is a gardener. In her younger and stronger years, she grew a variety of vegetables in vast amounts. Being passionate about her garden, she did not allow anyone in it without her accompanying them. I fondly remember my first time entering previously restricted areas without limitations. I was able to do that not because of who I was, but because I was there "in the name of my mother." My mother was with me, and she owned the garden! When we go before God in the name of Jesus, we are there because of who He is, and to accomplish His purpose.

Prayer is not a privilege or an option, but a command. It is the believer's spiritual contact with heaven. A positive, Spirit-filled life cannot be maintained without a powerful prayer life. There are various types of prayer with different functions. Following are selected types of prayer with descriptions.

" *Prayer is not a privilege or an option, but a command.* "

TYPES OF PRAYER

I am a woman of prayer, which does not mean my faith is always strong, but I believe nothing is too hard for God. *Intercessory prayer* is the type of prayer where I spend a great deal of time. Praying for concepts, groups, or individuals, and seeing the *fruit* or results of answered prayer confirms God's Word and strengthens my faith. Standing in the gap for others is a huge part of my personal ministry. Read below to discover the type of prayer to pray during specific times:

Prayer of Agreement: Jesus introduced the prayer of agreement when He said, "Again I say to you that if two of you agree on earth concerning anything that they ask, it will be done for them by My Father in heaven" (Matthew 18:19 NKJV). In order for the prayer of agreement to work, the people involved in the prayer must agree. To use the prayer of agreement, you must be sure that the person with whom you are agreeing is in line with what you are asking. You must make sure you know the specifics and that you are in perfect agreement about your prayer request before you join another believer in the prayer of agreement.

Prayer of Faith (supplication, salvation, petition): The prayer of faith is between you and God. It is you asking God for a particular outcome. The key verse for the prayer of faith is Mark 11:24, in which Jesus says, "Therefore I say to you, whatever things you ask when you pray, believe that you receive them, and you will have them" (NKJV). When you pray, you must believe that you have received your request. Hebrews 11:1 says, "Now faith is the substance of things hoped for, the evidence of things not seen." Your faith is substance—it is something real, something tangible. It is evidence of things you cannot see. When you pray in faith, God immediately gives you what you prayed for—in the spirit realm. In the natural realm, it may take time for the answer to manifest itself. God answers prayers, and He will answer your specific prayer in line with His Word. Your faith brings answered prayer out of the spiritual world into the physical world. How many times in Scripture does Jesus say to someone, "According to your faith"? When Jesus went to His hometown, "He did not do many mighty works there because of their unbelief" (Matthew 13:58). He referred to peoples' faith constantly. He always credited their faith, even though it was His power that healed them.

Prayer of Consecration and Dedication (commitment): In Luke 22:41–42, we see outlined the prayer of consecration and dedication: "And He was withdrawn from them about a stone's throw, and He knelt down and prayed, saying, 'Father, if it is Your will, take this cup away from Me; nevertheless not My will, but Yours, be done'" (NKJV). The key for Jesus, and for us, is, "Nevertheless not My will, but Yours, be done." In the absence of direct instructions, the prayer of consecration and dedication says you will allow God to set your direction or make your decisions. The prayer of consecration and dedication is appropriate when you have two (or more) godly alternatives before you, and you are not certain which direction God wants you to take.

Prayer of Praise and Worship (thanksgiving): In this prayer, you want to praise the Lord, to thank Him for His many blessings and His mercy. You want to tell Him how much you love Him. When we pray the prayer of faith, we should always include worship and praise. In Luke 18:43, the blind man who was healed was described as "glorifying God." The verse also says all the people who witnessed the miracle "gave praise to God." They prayed prayers of thanksgiving. Look at the way Jesus prayed in John 11:41: "Father, I thank You that You have heard Me," referring to His previous prayer regarding Lazarus. In the Lord's Prayer, Jesus told His disciples, "When you pray, say: Our Father in heaven, hallowed be Your name" (Luke 11:2). Paul wrote to the Philippians: "Be anxious for nothing, but in everything by prayer and supplication, with thanksgiving, let your requests be made known to God" (Philippians 4:6 NKJV).

Prayer of Intercession: Intercession means that you are acting in prayer on behalf of someone else. It may involve praying in a general way for such things as the church or the government, or offering up more specific prayers based on your knowledge of need. Often, I am asked to pray for others. This not only increases my prayer time, but it also increases my faith. In Ephesians 1:15–18, Paul wrote: "Therefore

I also, after I heard of your faith in the Lord Jesus and your love for all the saints, do not cease to give thanks for you, making mention of you in my prayers; that the God of our Lord Jesus Christ, the Father of glory, may give to you the spirit of wisdom and revelation in the knowledge of Him, the eyes of your understanding being enlightened; that you may know what is the hope of His calling, what are the riches of the glory of His inheritance in the saints" (NKJV). Here Paul makes it plain that he prayed regularly for the church at Ephesus and for the individuals there to receive these blessings. In Paul's greeting to the Philippians, he wrote, "I thank my God upon every remembrance of you, always in every prayer of mine making request for you all with joy" (Philippians 1:3–4 NKJV). The fact that Paul said he made requests for them suggests that this also was an example of *intercessory prayer.*

"

Your faith brings answered prayer out of the spiritual world into the physical world.

"

Prayer of Binding and Loosing: Pray that the Lord will loose angelic spirits to work on your behalf in those areas where God has already promised you results. You can bind foul spirits that are at work in people's lives. Binding and loosing are based on the authority God has granted in Scripture. This prayer is found in Matthew 18:18–19. Jesus says: "Assuredly, I say to you, whatever you bind on earth will be bound in heaven, and whatever you loose on earth will be loosed in heaven. Again I say to you that if two of you agree on earth concerning anything that they ask, it will be done for them by My Father in heaven" (NKJV). We have authority here on earth by our covenant rights through Jesus. Actions start here on earth. "Whatever you bind on earth will be bound in heaven, and whatever you loose on earth will be loosed in heaven." This prayer works only in line with God's Word and His laws. When you pray in this manner, God affirms it in heaven and puts His seal of approval on your prayer.

Additionally, it is important to set aside a quiet place and time for prayer. Spend a determined amount of time in silence—praying and meditating.

PLACES AND PRACTICES FOR PRAYER

As a former *Prayer Ministry Leader*, I can confirm the effectiveness of incorporating a variety of practices or methods to encourage church and community members to pray. Though our community has incorporated most practices at some point, the most successful practices in our congregation today are prayer calendars, prayer chains, drive-through prayer, and social media. Each practice brings something different to our minds. Each facet of a church's prayer life provides an opportunity for newcomers to step forward in faith. But your local church does not have to pursue every approach to prayer; it would then become "something to do" instead of *"something to be."* Just try one practice at a time and see how it takes hold. If a certain approach does not catch on, leave that one and go to another. You cannot force authentic prayer.

PRAYER WALKING YOUR NEIGHBORHOOD

Most churches feel somewhat disconnected from their neighborhoods. It is an almost sure bet that many people in your church's neighborhood think your church is aloof from them. Though hospital visitations are different from prayer walking, as a minister, I have prayed with numerous patients and their families. (Side note: *Remain cognizant that the person who may be in the sick bed is not the only family member in need of prayer.*) One of the many things churches are doing about this is prayer walking. The basic idea is that the church's prayer ministry team (and other concerned members) go in pairs to walk through various parts of the neighborhood and pray there. This may be:

- in front of the house of someone in material need;
- at a street crossing run by gangs, pimps, pushers, etc.;
- where people earn a living;
- where the local occultist followers gather;
- in front of each house or apartment building for the potential believers who live there;
- at roadside memorials, crime scenes, and cemeteries;
- near places where the powerful movers and shakers make their decisions;

- at places where violence and death rule;
- near schools.

Cell (area, zip, etc. codes or zones) groups within congregations also prayer walk, often involving two or three cells or prayer ministries in a section of town. Student groups at colleges and high schools can make a prayer stop a day at places in the school where trouble is most likely to happen. During their breaks, nurses can make stops in front of patients' rooms, out of their sight, praying for their health and faith. Wherever the pull against God is strong, that is where the prayer walking is done most regularly. It is to be done *as invisibly as possible*, so that those praying become part of the background. That way, if someone comes to you, it is purely a work of God and not due to your own attention-grabbing. Prayer walking is not done to be seen; it *is done to see*. Jesus warns us against that in Matthew 6:5.

Some writers describe prayer walking in terms of complex strategies of spiritual warfare and "territorial spirits" to claim victory over neighborhoods. But you do not have to think of it that way. The idea is really very simple: when you go to a place to pray for the people there, you are where the action is. You are not projecting. You are seeing your neighborhood in a different light. You will see the people and buildings and activities, and you may even see things happen as you are standing there. You will hear the sounds and smell the smells. In most churches, most of the people do not really know or care much about neighborhoods outside of their own. When you are actually on the scene, the meditations are clearer and more focused, and the prayers are more urgent and are much more likely to have a face or a life in mind. It gives you a chance to think of what place each activity has in the world and each person has in the kingdom of God. And after you have prayed there a while, you might actually feel the Spirit tugging on your mind, telling you what deeds you might be called on to do there. Someone might come up to you and ask for your prayers, or maybe your help.

DRIVE-THROUGH PRAYER

Drive-through prayer is similar to prayer walking. The major difference is that the recipients come to you. Once the strategic locations are identified, advertisements are prepared and posted to notify people that they can come to the place or places listed for personal or group prayer. More convenience is added by allowing attendees to remain in their vehicles while prayer team members pray.

You get real and keep it 100 percent! It may also help to take notes before recipients leave (or before you leave a spot), such as impressions, things for further prayer, and so on. Even if you only pray together with those you are with, you have taken a major step in loving the people there and in setting things spiritually right.

Prayer walks work best when there is a definite starting time and a definite ending time, when all the prayer walkers meet together. At the start, they talk together about any specific questions or tips, and have a joint prayer. Large groups break up and go to their areas. (It is okay if there is overlap.) At the end, groups should hold a semi-formal debriefing (S.W.O.T.—Strengths, Weaknesses, Opportunities, and Threats), sharing what they saw and experienced, and any new prayer concerns. Essential points to remember:

In prayer walks or drive-through prayers, we pray in detail, care in detail, learn in detail, and prayerfully, we listen to God in detail.

Another helpful practice is that of having a prayer team do a mini-prayer walk around the grounds of the church before anyone else arrives on Sunday or before other specified events. The team walks around the property of the church building, in the parking lot, along each row of seats in the sanctuary, then in the altar area, the pulpit, prayer stations, circulation desk, choir/band area, Sunday school classrooms, the fellowship hall, and the doorway, praying for those who will be in each of these places, that the Spirit will work in them and that lives will change for Christ. The tour usually ends with a prayer session with the minister and the worship leaders before the service begins.

PRAYER CALENDARS

Most people have a life that is so complex and hard to plan that they just can't get around to setting aside the time to pray about specific concerns of the congregation. Or they forget. For those people, a *prayer calendar* may be a useful tool. The prayer calendar can be in the church newsletter, at the information area, or be distributed electronically. On the prayer calendar, each day is set aside for a specific prayer regarding one specific matter, then the next day another prayer on another matter, then another on another matter, and so on. Below is a seven-day sample calendar (week):

1. discernment for the leadership team as it makes decisions;
2. the youth ministries;
3. the church in Belize, that they may reach those who do not believe;
4. the churches in New Orleans, coping with loss;
5. a new church being planted in Youngstown, Ohio;
6. a write-in day (for example: pray for peace in your relative's family);
7. the pastoral care ministry in your church.

The next week would have a different set of prayers tied to each day, covering the same wide span of things, universal to personal. (This way, the prayers stay balanced instead of narrowed down to one's own main interests or needs.)

PRAYER VIGILS

To be on a vigil is to be wakeful for a purpose. To the ancient Romans, that could mean to stand guard, spy on the activities of a possible enemy, or prepare for a holy occasion. Originally, the desire to take part in the holy occasion is so strong that you can't wait for it to happen, which means you are so full of determination that waiting and getting ready is *all* you can do, to the neglect of sleep or food. You do not want to miss a second of it; you want to be there at sunrise.

A *prayer* vigil (or prayer watch) happens when people get that way about praying. It can be done individually, but it is usually done by a group of people who set it up to make sure there is always someone praying. Today's vigils are done to hold a specific matter in prayer before God. Usually it is to prepare for a specific action, such as reaching out in witness for Christ, starting a ministry, making a major decision, or supporting a broader Christian ministry or mission. Traditional church vigils for holy days are not really prayer vigils, because so much more is involved, but they do contain much prayer.

To start a prayer vigil, someone has to want it passionately enough to get eight or more people to commit at the start. (These early joiners help shape and lead the vigil.) That group must decide what the vigil's focus will be, and stick to it. It is important to get the full support of a church pastor. Once that is done, it is a good idea to prepare a written guide that explains what a prayer vigil is (assume that the readers do not know), why this vigil is being done, how long it will run, and how they can take part in it. Also, it should tell readers who to talk to about it. Have one focal place for the vigil, where people know they can go to be part of it. This place can be a sanctuary or a prayer chapel, or even an outdoor site. The place must be fairly quiet, worshipful, and easy to get to. Many people can be there at any one time (in fact, plan that there would be times when many will be there), but someone should always be there for the entire vigil. Privately encourage those who can't make it there to pray at home, according to the guide's schedule. Try to involve prayer-people from other churches, especially those from churches that are not in partnership with your church.

An event of less than two hours is *not* much of a vigil, but a long prayer meeting. To state the obvious: a vigil takes *vigilance*—and should put your vigilance to the test and rise above limits.

" A prayer posture is a form of listening that invites prayer to come from a deeper place within. "

PRAYER CHAINS

Prayer chains are some of the most common prayer activities among congregations. The idea is simple: when there are prayer needs in the congregation, rather than wait until Sunday, begin praying for them immediately by spreading the concerns by way of the telephone or text message. It is simple, and almost everyone has the time to do it. How do I begin one in my church?

(1) Ask around.

- See if a prayer chain exists already. If one does, join it, and talk to its coordinator/leader about its expansion.
- Most active churchgoers already know what a prayer chain is, though most of them have never been part of one. Tell the people in the worship services, Bible studies, and small groups that you are starting one.
- While there should be at least a few people who have a mature faith, it is also a good idea to include a few newcomers. Invite the members who drop their children off for Sunday school and leave. Or invite someone who is giving or receiving services from the church.

(2) Create prayer chain "trees"—a paper outline of who will pass the prayer requests to whom, with names and phone numbers. Each "branch" should have at least three and no more than ten people on it; when there is more, create a new branch. This tree, with numbers, is to be given to each member of the chain.

(3) The chain coordinator/leader calls the first person on each branch with the message. The first one on the branch passes it to the next. If that person is unavailable, try the next one on that branch until you talk to an actual person and pass the requests along, and that person should pass it on to the next person on the branch. When passing along the requests, specifically say, "I'm calling for the prayer chain, and these are our current requests …" Then relay the message. Then end the call with a "Good-bye" or "God bless."

(4) NO CHATTING and NO ADDING DETAILS beyond those passed along. PERIOD. Chatting and added details should have no part in a prayer chain (James 1:26). It is true of male and female—young and old alike: the more talk, the more gossip. If you know (or think you know) further details, keep them

to yourself, no matter how strong the urge is to share them. It is the chain coordinator/leader's responsibility to speak to the person requesting prayer (or the person being prayed for) about what to tell the prayer chain, when there is a question. If an additional detail is not in the message, assume there is a reason it is not. Stick strictly to the message. Also, no word should be spread on or off the chain about who *asked* for the prayer; *that, too, is private information.* Such privacy or tight limits may not sound friendly, but my experience is that privacy is extremely important (Psalm 141:3).

SOCIAL MEDIA

As a counseling intern, it was mandatory for me to become "highly wired." It helped me to remain connected with my classmates, clients, instructor, and supervisor. Social media became my friend. If you have a group of people who are highly wired (for example, they have email or Facebook messaging and use it more than once a day), then email or messaging can be a good way to chain them together, by way of a formal group. This has the advantage of more easily involving former members and interested people in distant places and time zones. Facebook groups or pages are usually too publicly accessible for use by a prayer chain. However, Facebook groups (not pages) have been used well for a particular ongoing request where the request or the news is open to the public. The Facebook group then acts as a chain for news and prayer updates on that specific request, and new people may be added to that group over time as needed or requested. Additionally, prayers may be prayed through phone calls (conference or emergency situations), texting, and Twitter. Twitter has shown itself especially useful for quick, brief, arrow-type (shoot straight to the point) breath prayers, pass-alongs (when the arrow prayer is passed on to another, who passes it on to still more people) and urgent situations (such as auto accidents and critical illnesses).

PRAYER POSTURE

"Bow your head and close your eyes." In a small traditional church, that was the phrase I used countless times. Why? It is the posture I was taught as a child. Paying attention to our posture and letting it help guide and focus our prayer can move us to pray powerfully. While we can make prayer one of the many things we multitask during our day, such as while driving, cleaning, or waiting in line, we *need to set aside some time when all we do is PRAY*. Adding a posture or series of postures to our prayer helps us to make a total commitment, resulting in a fuller connection with God. Our responses can help guide us to body postures and movements which may embrace or enhance our connection to God. A prayer posture is a form of listening that invites prayer to come from a deeper place within. Putting the body in a particular position can stimulate uniquely powerful prayer. Also, prayer posture gives access to prayer when words fail. By adopting a posture based on how you feel at the moment, you are able to present yourself to God with an authenticity that is different from words. The following prayer postures are recorded or indicated in the Holy Bible:

a. lying prostrate on the ground with arms outstretched: Matthew 26:39; Mark 14:35

b. arms stretched upward—lifting up hands: 1 Timothy 2:8

c. kneeling down: Luke 22:41; Acts 7:60, 9:40, 20:36, 21:5; Ephesians 3:14

d. head bowed with hands folded: 2 Chronicles 6:13; Daniel 6:10

e. standing: Mark 11:25

f. sitting with hands extended, palms up, resting backs of the hands on the thighs: 2 Samuel 7:18

HINDRANCES TO POWERFUL PRAYER

Think of your prayer life as a body part which needs exercise to be strengthened. A few years ago, I broke my ankle. Being a fitness advocate, I was limited in the exercises I was able to do. After I was consistent with my physical therapy, soon (but not as soon as I wanted) my ankle was strengthened; I was able to climb the mountain again and resume my walks. Having a broken ankle was a hindrance to my exercise routine. Maintaining consistency in my exercises proved very effective in my healing process. It is apparent to me that God desires all of us to maintain consistent and effective prayer lives. Examine your prayer life to determine if there are factors preventing your prayers from being answered. Pray for the obstacles to be removed; soon you will be able to connect with God on a higher level. Following are the most common hindrances to an effective prayer life:

Known Sin—This is probably the most common prayer killer. Why pray powerless prayers? Scripture tells us that God is perfect and can't abide sin in us. If we knowingly tolerate sin in our lives, it pushes God away from us. As a result, it makes our prayers powerless. Read Psalm 66:16–18.

Willful Disobedience to God's Word—Obedience should be a natural outgrowth of faith in God. He that obeys God trusts Him; he that trusts Him obeys Him. If we are to grow in our relationship with God and become strong people of prayer, we must learn to obey. Having faith alone is not enough; neither is keeping free from sin. See Proverbs 28:9.

Lack of Genuine Faith—The lack of faith has a tremendous impact on the life of a Christian. Lack of faith makes a person incapable of hearing or receiving from God. Without faith, prayer has no power. Furthermore, the faithless should not expect to receive anything from the Lord. See James 1:6–8.

Selfish Motivation—Know your motive before you pray, then go before God with a pure heart. If not, your motives will be exposed. When our motives are not right in prayer, our prayers have no power. See Matthew 6:5.

Idols in the Heart—Do you have anything in your life that you would not release to God? Examine your relationships with *persons, possessions, or professions*. If God asks, would you give it up? When idols are removed from our lives, we enter into personal revival with God. See 1 Corinthians 8:4.

Unforgiving Spirit—Bitterness comes from unforgiveness. There is no way a person can enter prayer with bitterness and exit with blessings. When a person forgives another, they are forgiven by the Father. See Matthew 5:23–24.

Hypocrisy—When you want to experience spiritual, physical, and emotional restoration, live a transparent life. Transparency shows others that they are not alone in their challenges. When we confess our sins to one another, which requires us to be absolutely transparent, God is able to heal and cleanse us. See 1 John 1:5–9.

Discord in Home Relationships—Prayer helps you to show compassion to others. You cannot pray for a person and criticize them at the same time. God's desire for all believers (between Christian brothers and sisters, husbands and wives, lay people and pastors) is unity. Prayer does not support competition but compassion. See 1 Peter 3,4.

Unsurrendered Will—Do not hold on to what belongs to God. When you surrender totally, the result will be tremendous fruit. There are great benefits of surrendering your will to God. One is that God promises to answer your prayers and grant your requests. Additionally, you get *to receive the power of Christ through the Holy Spirit. God flows through us, gives us power, and produces fruit.* See John 15:7–8.

Denying God's Sovereignty—It is clear that God is in charge, as He taught the disciples how to pray. It also establishes our relationship to Him: that of a child under the authority of his Father. Anytime we deny the divine order of things, we are out of bounds, and we hinder our relationship with our heavenly Father. See Matthew 6.

.

" Prayer helps you to show compassion to others "

LET US PRAY
—SPECIFIC PRAYERS

PRAYER FOR WISDOM

Father,

I pray for _____ that he/
she ____ might have wisdom. Keep him/her from
following the path of least resistance, and from people
who will lead them astray. Teach them that the path
of wisdom is often the most difficult path, but the
most rewarding. Keep them from ungodly counsel
that appears good, but that will be destructive. Make
us lovers of Your wisdom.

I pray that You will give me the heart of wisdom,
and I pray I will always make wise choices. When two
paths appear equal, I pray that You will help me to
trust You as I make my decision. I pray for a heart that
is willing to obey You and to respond in the faith and
wisdom that You give me. Order our paths, for we are
Your sheep and we hear Your voice. And it is so.

In Jesus' name,
Amen.
(See also 1 Kings 3.)

PRAYER FOR NATIONS

Father,

We thank You that Jesus is the light of the world. He said that whosoever follows Him shall not walk in darkness but have the light of life. Father, we thank You that Jesus is anointed to remove every burden and to destroy every yoke over our nation. He also sent that same anointing, the powerful Holy Spirit, to live and abide in us and to be with us forever. Father, we thank You for the anointing of the Holy Ghost, and the anointing to pray and to intercede for our nation today.

We come to stand in the gap and repent for all of Your people, as Daniel and Ezra did. Father, we repent, for we have sinned, we have transgressed Your laws, we have committed iniquity, we have done wickedly in Your sight. Father, we repent of the rebellion, idolatry, greed, perverseness, immorality, violence, and every wicked deed. We repent for taking You out of our schools and government and not putting You first in our lives. We repent for the wickedness that has come upon our nation and we ask that You convict every heart to confess and bring forth the truth of what happened and who is responsible.

We hallow Your holy name and we thank You that You loved us so much that You gave Your only begotten Son, that whoever shall believe in Him shall not perish, but have everlasting life. We thank You, Father, that Jesus was the Lamb of God, who took away the sins of the world. He was wounded for our transgressions, He was bruised for our iniquity, the chastisement of our peace was upon Him, and by His stripes we are healed.

Father, we thank You for this day, that we can stand in the gap and make up a hedge around our nation and this world so that evil deeds can be deterred. We praise You in advance for saved souls. We honor and adore You. And it is so.

In Jesus' name,
Amen.

PRAYER FOR ADULTS

Father,

I magnify Your name; I adore and love You. Please hide me behind the cross and allow me to abide in the shadows of the almighty. I pray that Your servants will skillfully develop the abilities and knowledge You have given them. Please instruct and guide us in how and what to teach, so we may prepare in advance for the youth. Continue to lead and guide us into Your truth. Help us to have stronger relationships with You. Help us to see the importance of ministering to youth. Thank You for joy so we will not grow weary in well-doing. Guide us to follow Your path and uphold godliness. Thank You for a daily walk with You. If God be for us, who can be against us? You said that You will give shepherds according to our heart. I ask You to give us hearts of love for children and youth. Inspire and anoint us to feed Your children the truth from Your Word. Grant us a fresh anointing of Your wisdom, understanding, power, knowledge, and joy. Give us hearts of compassion and love, and help us to grow. The Good Shepherd gives His life for the sheep. Help us to lay down our lives. And it is so.

In the name of Jesus, we pray,
Amen.

A MARRIAGE PRAYER

Father,

I come boldly before Your throne of grace in the name of Jesus to find help in the time of trouble in marriages. Lord, Your Word says that You are a very present help in the time of trouble. Oh God, You said that what You have joined together, let no man put asunder, or separate. So in the name that is above every name, in the name of JESUS, I come against every demonic force and spirit, I pull down every strong hold, I cancel and loose you, Satan, from your assignment. I take authority over every principality and spiritual wickedness in high places, in the name of JESUS. Father, I thank You that the weapons of our warfare are not carnal, but are mighty through You to the pulling down of strong holds. I enter into this strong man's house and take back JOY, PEACE, LOVE, and every good thing God has promised for my marriage. And it is so.

In Jesus' name,
Amen.

PRAYER FOR YOUTH

Father,

I am thankful that You will never leave Your children or reject them. Confirm to our children that You are a help for them. Thank You for Your angels who are always around our children, just because You are their God. Bring them to the knowledge that Your angels watch over them day and night and that Jesus lives in their hearts. Manifest in their every thought, so they will think only on those things which are pure and holy. Your Word is encouraging and will not allow them to be discouraged. There is nothing that can separate us from the love of Christ. Reassure Your children that they will always come out on top of every circumstance through Jesus' love. I decree love, joy, and peace in their lives. I speak to every demonic spirit and command them to GO! The haughty spirit must go; lust, lying, alcoholism, drug abuse—ALL must go, NOW!

I decree victorious lives. You gave Your Son for them; help them to live wholly for You … In the name that is above all others, the omnipotent and matchless name of Jesus, we pray. And it is so.
Amen.

STUDENTS' PRAYER

Father,

We stand in the gap for students of all ages. We decree supernatural excellence and success in every academic area. We pray for their presentation and preparation; whether they are taking standardized or teacher-made tests, we call on You, Holy Ghost, to be their helper. Reward their efforts, and help them to properly prepare and to retain what they have studied and what they have gleaned. Clear their minds of distractions and help them to remain focused on their task at hand. I pray that You will give them peace, wisdom, and knowledge. I pray that they will put this knowledge to good use in their lives and in the lives of those whom they will influence and touch during life's journey. I pray that You will give them direction for the future as You anoint, protect, guide, teach, and direct in all areas of their lives. Direct them to Your truth, and I pray that they will honor You in all that they do and say. Thank You for Your help and guidance. And it is so!

In Jesus' name,
Amen.

PERSONAL PRAYER

Father,

I pray that the Spirit of the Lord shall rest upon
_____. The spirit of wisdom and
understanding, the spirit of counsel and might, the
spirit of knowledge. We pray that as Your Spirit
rests upon _____, You will make him
of quick understanding because You, Lord, have
anointed and qualified him/her. _____
has been sent to bind up the brokenhearted and to
proclaim liberty to the physical and spiritual captives,
and the opening of the prison and of the eyes to
those who are bound.

_____ shall be called the priest of the Lord.
He/she shall eat the wealth of the nations. No weapon
that is formed against _____ shall
prosper, and any tongue that rises up in judgment shall
be shown to be in the wrong. We declare that Your
child holds fast and follows the pattern of wholesome
and sound teaching, in all faith and love, which is for
us, Christ Jesus. Father, we pray and believe each day,
freedom of utterance, _____ will
open his/her mouth, boldly and courageously, as he/

she ought. Thank You, Father, for what is already done. And it is so!

In Jesus' name,
Amen.

Harriet Gordon, LPC

CONCLUSION: FOCUS POINTS TO REMEMBER

BIBLE STUDY FOR POWERFUL PRAYER

Prayer produces power: *Use guides, and the Holy Bible, as the main resources to petition God for known requests.*

Purify yourself before you begin to pray: Numbers 19:12–20

Pray responsively: 1 Samuel 20:29; 1 Thessalonians 5

Stay tuned in to the promptings of the Holy Ghost: Isaiah 55:8; Proverbs 3

Pray with thanksgiving: Psalm 100:4; Philippians 4:6–7

Always pray with a thankful heart: Colossians 3:15; James 1:17

Pray in faith: Hebrews 11:6; James 5:15; Jude 1:20

God can do more than you can think or even ask: Mark 11:24; Ephesians 3:20

Pray in the Spirit: 1 Corinthians 14:14–15; Romans 8:26–27

Pray and praise in your gift of tongues: Ephesians 6:11–24

Pray fervently, as if the world depends upon it: Colossians 4:12; 1 Thessalonians 3:10; James 5:16–18

With bold confidence: Hebrews 4:16 (boldly, not brashly)

With reverence: Isaiah 66:2; Psalm 111:9, 89:7

With sincerity and selfless intent: Matthew 6:5–8

With humility: Luke 18:9–14; James 4:6,10; 1 Peter 5:6–7; 2 Chronicles 7:14, 34:27; Isaiah 57:15

Keeping alert (do not let your mind drift): Colossians 4:2; Luke 21:36

In Jesus' name: John 14:13–14, 15:16, 16:24,26; Colossians 3:17 (an attitude that we *pray by the authority of Jesus,* not merely saying the words, "In Jesus' name, amen")

Be devoted (make it a habit): Colossians 4:2; Romans 12:12; Acts 6:4

Have an attitude of thanksgiving: Colossians 4:2

With a forgiving spirit: Matthew 6:12–15; Matthew 18:21–35; Ephesians 4:32

With perseverance/persistence: Luke 11:5–9; Ephesians 6:18

Do not lose heart: Luke 18:1

Pray specifically: When ordering at a restaurant we do not say, "Bring food," but "I would like grilled salmon, medium-rare with lemon sauce, potato with sour cream, and hold the butter," etc.

Pray expecting to receive: Mark 11:24; 2 Samuel 22:7; James 1:5–8; Psalm 5:1–3

PRAY YOUR WAY TO EXCELLENT HEALTH

PRACTICE. Practice the principle outlined in the following words: "They that wait upon the Lord shall renew their strength" (Isaiah 40:31). This means stay close to God and Christ, and your strength will constantly be renewed, so that you will "mount up with wings as eagles . . . run, and not be weary . . . walk, and not faint."

PROFESS. Profess the perfection of your own creation. God made you, and He never did a bad piece of workmanship. Visualize your mental, physical, and spiritual organism as a perfect example of God's creation.

ABOUT THE AUTHOR

HARRIET GORDON serves on the Board of Elders at Light of the World Christian Tabernacle International Headquarters in Stockbridge, Georgia. She specializes in designing and leading transformational train-the-trainer developmental practices, and has received numerous awards for her successes. She is an Intercessor and leader in the Prayer Department, where she is an integral part and an active member. She has more than 35 years of experience in the Helps Ministry. She presently serves as advisor and Elder of the Youth Department, which serves youth and young adults ranging in age from infancy through 30. Harriet is an education advocate with more than 35 years of experience as a teacher and counselor. She is passionate about serving others. This is evident in her support roles, as she prays and donates time and resources in areas of research on aging, ADHD, teen violence, cancer, and other intervention/prevention studies. She is married to Glenn D. Gordon and they have two anointed adult offsprings, Isaac and Dawn (Jeremiah

Smith, son-in-love), with two adorable grandsons. This is Harriet's first professional publication. Be assured that more great publications will come from **Harriet Gordon, LPC.**